SOFRITO

A collection of recipes from
traditional to innovative

Devin Lukachik

Contents

What is Sofrito?

Sofrito is a deep and complex flavor base that forms the foundation of many dishes, such as rice, beans, soups and stews. It would be nearly impossible to pinpoint the exact origins of sofrito, as it has evolved in diverse ways within different cultures. While there is no way to be certain, it is widely believed to have originated in Spain, from its predecessor sofregit. Spanish sofregit typically consisted of tomatoes, onions, garlic, and sometimes peppers, slowly cooked in olive oil. With the colonization of the Americas, Spanish culinary traditions, including sofregit, made their way to Latin America. There, it began to transform as other indigenous crops were incorporated into the cooking base, resulting in the development of regional variations based on local preferences and availability of ingredients.

While these regional variations exist, sofrito can also vary by personal preference. After all, sofrito is not just a cooking technique- it holds cultural significance for many households and larger communities. It is often considered a representation of the fusion of indigenous, African, and European culinary influences, reflecting the diverse history and heritage of the people who use it in their cooking. In modern gastronomy, sofrito has transcended its traditional boundaries and is embraced by chefs and home cooks globally. This book contains a collection of many of the most typical and widespread types of sofrito, as well as some contemporary innovations. It also pays homage to other cooking bases around the world that may have evolved from or alongside sofrito.

How to Use These Recipes

Sofrito is not just the name of a dish, but of a cooking style. It comes from the Spanish word *sofreír*, meaning to fry in hot oil. Thus, it should be understood that nearly all of the recipes in this book, unless indicated, should be cooked *sofrito*- broken down into small components and fried for several minutes to release their flavors.

How the ingredients in these recipes are broken down can be a matter of preference. Some choose to finely chop or dice sofrito ingredients, while others opt to use a food processor or blender for a finer mixture. Either way, the process is the same- first, break down the ingredients as small as you prefer; second, sautée the mixture in oil or fat; and third, use the aromatic mixture that results as a building block for your dishes.

It is common practice in many countries to complete the first step ahead of time, chopping or blending a large batch of ingredients and saving it in a jar or container, and then taking spoonfuls at a time to fry them when the time comes to cook. With this method, most uncooked sofritos will last in the fridge for several weeks.

Another common tradition is to prepare the raw sofrito and freeze it into cubes using an ice cube tray, keeping them in the freezer to conveniently add one or two cubes to your pan when cooking. This method preserves the sofrito for much longer and can be a great time-saver.

No matter the method, it's always ideal to have some sofrito on hand. The recipes in this book vary in terms of the amount they yield, but they can be adjusted to make as small or large a batch as one desires.

Basic Sofritos

These sofritos are simple, traditional, and comforting, but that doesn't make them any less delicious. These basic recipes have some of the most versatile applications and can even serve as building blocks for other kinds.

3-Ingredient Sofrito Blanco

This recipe is as simple as they come, and focuses on humble, aromatic alliums to pack it full of flavor. Aside from the salt and oil, it only uses three household ingredients.

-2 white onions

-12 garlic cloves

-2 shallots

-Olive oil and salt to taste

Yields: 3 cups

Use for:

-White rice

-Steamed mussels

-Add to canned beans

Classic Sofrito

This is a timeless version of sofrito, and similar types can be found in Costa Rica and throughout Central and South America.

-3 yellow onions

-8 cloves of garlic

-1 red bell pepper

-1 green bell pepper

-Olive oil or butter and salt to taste

Yields: 5 cups

Use for:

-Rice dishes

-Beans

-Pan-seared or stewed meats

Traditional Spanish Sofrito

Spanish sofrito is a bit different from the Latin American varieties. It usually contains tomato and paprika and is often cooked down before storing. You can choose to cook the sofrito ingredients before you store them, or store the mixture raw and cook a spoonful at a time when you make your dishes.

-2 yellow onions

-2 medium tomatoes

-1 red bell pepper

-1 green bell pepper

-4 garlic cloves

-1 ½ tablespoons of sweet Spanish paprika

-2 tablespoons of tomato paste

-Olive oil and salt to taste

Yields: 4.5 cups

Use for:

-Paella

-Braised meats

-Stews

Spanish Sofrito with Saffron

This delicious sofrito, designed for paella, features aromatic saffron to add even more layers of flavor. For another traditional version that incorporates meat, see page 52.

- 1 yellow onion

- 1 red bell pepper

- 1 yellow bell pepper

- 5 garlic cloves

- 3 shallots

- 2 tablespoons of tomato paste

- 1 tablespoon of sweet Spanish paprika

- 2 tablespoons of Spanish sherry vinegar

- 2 tablespoons of dry white wine (cooking wine or otherwise)

- ¼ cup of vegetable stock

- 2 bay leaves, finely ground

- Leaves of 3 sprigs of thyme (or ½ tablespoon dried thyme)

- 9 saffron threads

- Olive oil and salt to taste

Yields: 4.5 cups

Use for:

- Paella

- Spanish rice

- Stews

Puerto Rican Sofrito (Recaíto)

This traditional Puerto Rican sofrito features delicious ají dulce peppers, which are sweet and have a mild heat, and recao, also called culantro. If you can't find some of these ingredients, try out the simplified recaíto on the following page.

- 3 yellow onions

- 2 green bell peppers

- 1 bunch of cilantro

- 1 bunch of culantro

- 10 garlic cloves

- 12 to 15 ají dulce peppers

- ½ of a red bell pepper

- 1 teaspoon of achiote

- Olive oil and salt to taste

Yields: 6.5 cups

Use for:

- Arroz con gandules

- Red beans

- Roast pork

Recaíto Sencillo

Where traditional recaíto ingredients may be difficult to obtain, this recipe mimics some of that Puerto Rican flavor with sweet cubanelle peppers. The culantro is also omitted, but you can add some if you have it.

-2 yellow onions

-2 green bell peppers

-1 red bell pepper

-3 cubanelle peppers

-6 garlic cloves

-1 banana pepper

-1 bunch of cilantro

-Olive oil and salt to taste

Yields: 4.5 cups

Use for:

-Arroz con gandules

-Stewed meats

-Plantain dishes

Recaíto with Alcaparrado

Alcaparrado is a Spanish condiment sometimes added to sofritos in Puerto Rico. It adds a briny, savory punch to your dishes. Alcaparrado can be purchased already made, or you can make your own by combining manzanilla olives, capers, and pimientos. The ratios of this version are a bit different from the other recaítos and result in a stronger flavor that complements the olives. Olive oil and salt aren't needed here because of the brine from the alcaparrado.

-3 yellow onions

-3 green bell peppers

-3 red bell peppers

-1 whole head of garlic

-2 8-oz jars of alcaparrado (or 2/3 cup olives, 2/3 cup capers, ½ cup pimientos)

-2 bunches of cilantro

-2 bunches of cilantro

Yields: 10-12 cups

Use for:

-Sauces

-Marinades

-Rice dishes

Basic Dominican Sofrito (Sazón)

This pungent sofrito is typically made with vinegar and red onion and adds a wonderful acidity to dishes.

- 1 red onion

- 1 tablespoon of apple cider vinegar

- 1 red bell pepper

- 1 green bell pepper

- ½ bunch of culantro

- ½ bunch of cilantro (use whole bunch if omitting culantro)

- 8 cloves of garlic

- 1 teaspoon of achiote

- 1 teaspoon of oregano

- Olive oil and salt to taste

Yields: 4.5 cups

Use for:

- Red beans

- Marinades

- Fish

Sazón Rojo

Some Dominicans make sazón with tomatoes, creating a sweeter sofrito, like this one with plenty of achiote and onion.

-2 red onions

-3 tablespoons of achiote

-1 red bell pepper

-1 yellow bell pepper

-1 radish

-2 tablespoons of apple cider vinegar

-Juice of half a lime

-1 tablespoon of naranja agria

-2 tablespoons of tomato paste

-2 large tomatoes

- ½ bunch of cilantro

-8 cloves of garlic

- ¼ cup of pimientos

-Olive oil and salt to taste

Yields: 5 cups

Use for:

-Red beans

-Stews

-Rice dishes

Sazón Verde

Every Dominican sazón differs a bit and is often a household recipe. This is a more herbal green version that pairs well with seafood.

-1 red onion

-1 green bell pepper

-1 yellow bell pepper

-1 bunch of cilantro

-1 bunch of cilantro

-½ stalk of celery

-6 cloves of garlic

-1 ½ tablespoons of oregano

-1 ½ teaspoons of thyme

-1 ají dulce pepper or 2 cubanelle peppers

-Juice of ½ a lime

-Olive oil and salt to taste

Yields: 5 cups

Use for:

-Shrimp

-Fish

-Plantain dishes

Colombian Sofrito (Hogao)

This simple Colombian creole sauce is cooked down into a rich and aromatic sofrito used as a base for many delicious dishes or served on the side as a sauce.

-5 medium or 3 large tomatoes

-1 bunch of green onions

-½ of a white onion

-Olive oil and salt to taste

Yields: 4-5 cups

Use for:

-Yuca fries

-Arepas

-Stews

Spiced Hogao

Hogao can be prepared many different ways, and while the traditional version is delicious in its simplicity, this one features added aromatics and spices for a complex taste.

-9 medium or 6 large tomatoes

-2 bunches of green onions

-1 bunch of cilantro

-1 whole head of garlic

-3 shallots

-1 tablespoon of oregano

-1 tablespoon of smoked paprika

-2 tablespoons of cumin

-1 tablespoon of parsley

-1 bouillon cube (chicken or vegetable) or equivalent

-Olive oil and salt to taste

Yields: 10 cups

Use for:

-Arepas

-Plantain dishes

-Braised meats

Cuban Sofrito

A good Cuban sofrito is a critical base for arroz con pollo, fricasé, and more. For another traditional version that includes pork, see page 54.

-1 white onion

-1 red bell pepper

-1 green bell pepper

-1 cubanelle pepper (can substitute with poblano)

-1 fresh tomato or 1 cup diced tomato

-1 tablespoon tomato paste or 3 tablespoons tomato sauce

-8 cloves of garlic

-¼ cup of white wine (cooking wine or otherwise)

-2 bay leaves, finely ground

-1 tablespoon of oregano

-1 teaspoon of cumin

-1 teaspoon of smoked paprika

-Olive oil and salt to taste

Yields: 5 cups

Use for:

-Arroz con pollo

-Fricasé de Pollo

-Ropa vieja

Chilean Coloring Oil

This quick infused oil is a staple in Chilean kitchens and is used just like a sofrito to serve as a base for sautéed dishes, adding a rich red color and deep flavor. It includes a special chili powder called merkén, which is made from the cacho de cabra pepper in Chile. It can be found online or in some specialty stores, but you can omit it or substitute for other chili powders, especially ones that use other dark and fruity smoked peppers. Simply fry the whole garlic cloves and toast the seasonings in the hot fat, then strain, cool and store.

-2 cups of lard (can use shortening or canola oil if necessary, but lard is more typical)

-3 tablespoons of quality paprika

-3 tablespoons of merkén (or substitute with another dark smoky chili powder and a pinch of toasted coriander seeds)

-5 cloves of garlic

-1 shallot (optional)

Yields: 2 cups

Use for:

-Marinating meats

-Rice dishes

-Sautéed vegetables

Sofrito Criollo

Variations of this sofrito can be found all throughout Central and South America. It is versatile and dependable in any dish, while still packing lots of flavor.

-2 medium tomatoes

-1 red bell pepper

-1 green bell pepper

-1 bunch of cilantro

-2 yellow onions

-2 cloves of garlic

-1 ½ tablespoons of sugar

-3 tablespoons of tomato paste

-1 tablespoon of apple cider vinegar

-1 tablespoon of oregano

-1 teaspoon of parsley

-1 teaspoon of onion powder

-1 teaspoon of garlic powder

Yields: 6 cups

Use for:

-Beans

-Rice dishes

-Stewed meats

Sofrito con Albahaca

This sofrito contains flavorful basil for a unique taste that pairs well with poultry or as an addition to sauces. If you happen to have pasta de albahaca (a basil paste common in Perú and other countries) leftover from another recipe, you can add it or use it in place of fresh basil.

-1 yellow onion

-1 cup of fresh basil leaves

-1 green bell pepper

-4 cloves of garlic

- ½ bunch of cilantro

-1 tablespoon of tomato paste

-1 teaspoon of sugar

-1 tablespoon of lime juice

-1 shallot

-Olive oil and salt to taste

Yields: 3.5 cups

Use for:

-Sauces

-Marinating meats

-Arroz con pollo

Ecuadorian Refrito/Hogo

This simple sofrito works brilliantly with potatoes and other vegetables.

-1 white onion

-3 cloves of garlic

-3 tablespoons of achiote

-1 teaspoon of cumin

-1 bay leaf, finely ground

-Olive oil and salt to taste

Yields: 1.5-2 cups

Use for:

-Corn

-Potatoes

-Beans

Aderezo

Aderezo is the base of a wide variety of dishes in Peruvian cuisine. This classic version features delicious ají amarillo peppers, a widely used Peruvian pepper renowned for its flavor. While fresh or frozen may or may not be available depending where one lives, jars of ají amarillo paste are usually easy to find and make an excellent substitute. Red onion is also traditional to this recipe and Peruvian cuisine in general.

-1 whole head of garlic

-3 red onions

-8-10 ají amarillo peppers or 1 jar of ají amarillo paste

-Olive oil, canola oil, or lard, and salt to taste

Yields: 5 cups

Use for:

-Peruvian rice dishes

-Stews

-White beans

Aderezo Costeño

This aderezo from the northern coasts of Perú includes ají panca, which much like ají amarillo, can be readily found in many places as a paste. It also contains zapallo loche, a nutty type of squash which can be substituted for pumpkin or butternut squash.

-5 red onions

-1 whole head of garlic

-15 ají panca peppers or 1 jar of ají panca paste

-1 zapallo loche, butternut squash, or small pumpkin

-½ bunch of culantro

-Olive oil (or lard) and salt to taste

Yields: 10 cups

Use for:

-Arroz con pato

-Stewed meats

-Shrimp dishes

Aderezo con Cilantro

Peruvian cilantro paste is a very common addition to aderezo, especially in the North of Perú. It is a vital component of many traditional Peruvian stews. Of course, while cilantro paste is typical, fresh cilantro can easily be substituted.

-4 red onions

-1 whole head of garlic

-1 jar of cilantro paste or 1 bunch each of cilantro and culantro

-1 cup of peruvian peppers (ají amarillo, ají panca, ají dulce or a combination) or 4 tablespoons of the pepper paste of your choosing

-Olive oil (or lard) and salt to taste

Yields: 6 cups

Use for:

-Aguadito de pollo

-Seco de carne

-Rice dishes

Sofrito Guatemalteco para Hilachas

This vibrant sofrito is a traditional base for hilachas, a Guatemalan beef stew, but can also be used to spice up potatoes, vegetables, legumes, and more.

-2-3 medium tomatoes or 1 large can

-8 tomatillos

-5 dried guajillo chilis

-1 yellow onion

-6 cloves of garlic

Yields: 3 cups

Use for:

-Hilachas

-Sautéed vegetables

-Beans

Refogado/Estrugido

In Brazil and Portugal, refogado or estrugido is used in a wide variety of dishes to enhance their flavor. It is often cooked down and then made into a rather thick paste, so not much olive oil is needed.

-1 yellow onion

-6 cloves of garlic

-Olive oil to taste

Yields: 1.5 cups

Use for:

-Rice

-Feijoada

-Stewed meats

Tempero Pronto

An enhanced Brazilian refogado that is ready to season anything and everything.

-2 yellow onions

-10 cloves of garlic

-1 bunch of green onions

-1 bunch of parsley

-Olive oil, salt, and black pepper to taste

Yields: 5 cups

Use for:

-Rice

-Moqueca Baiana

-Sauces

Sofrito for Mexican Rice

A classic aromatic sofrito typically used to make rice dishes more flavorful.

-½ yellow onion

-4 cloves of garlic

-1 medium tomato

-1 tablespoon of tomato paste or 1 cube of tomato bouillon

-Neutral oil and salt to taste

Yields: 1 cup

Use for:

-Mexican rice

-Arroz con pollo

-Soups

Nontraditional Sofritos

These sofritos may not be as typical, but they are designed to transform and elevate food. They are innovations of the standard types of sofritos that have evolved all over the world.

Chayote Sofrito

The chayote fruit is a healthy and delicious addition to sofrito. When cooked down and blended into the sauce, it adds a subtle sweetness and nuttiness that balances out some of the sharper flavors.

-Meat of 1 chayote

-1 yellow onion

-4 cloves of garlic

-1 green bell pepper

-½ bunch of cilantro

-1 cube of bouillon (chicken or vegetable)

-Zest and juice of 1 lemon

-Butter or olive oil and salt to taste

Yields: 3 cups

Use for:

-Soups

-Sautéed vegetables

-Sauce for poultry

Sweet Corn Sofrito

Another vegetable-based variety, the corn in this sofrito makes it thick and sweet. Any kind of corn will do well in this recipe, but using a few different heirloom varieties will really boost the flavor. Use butter instead of oil for a delightful richness.

-Kernels from 4 ears of corn (or 2 cans worth)

-1 yellow onion

-1 red onion or shallot

-6 cloves of garlic

-1 bunch of cilantro

-3 poblano peppers

-1 green bell pepper

-Zest and juice of 1 lime

-2 tablespoons of sugar

-2 tablespoons of ají amarillo paste (optional)

-Butter and salt to taste

Yields: 6-8 cups

Use for:

-Rice dishes

-Soups

-Incorporate into masa

Mango Habanero Sofrito

While mango and habanero are a classic pairing for salsas, they also make a great sofrito. Allow the mango to cook down considerably before blending into a fine paste.

- 4 small or 2 large mangos

- 8-12 habaneros, depending on spice preference

- 1 yellow onion

- 1 red bell pepper

- ½ bunch of cilantro

- 2 serrano peppers

- 1 clove of garlic

- 1 tablespoon of sugar

- 1 tablespoon of smoked paprika

- Zest of 1 lime or ½ an orange (optional)

- 1 teaspoon of turmeric

- Butter or olive oil and salt to taste

Yields: 5-6 cups

Use for:

- Sauces

- Rice dishes

- Marinating seafood

Peach Poblano Sofrito

Another fruity twist on sofrito, sweet with a mild kick. Like the mango one, you'll want to cook down the peaches until very soft before blending.

-Flesh of 3 peaches, any variety

-6 poblano peppers

-2 serrano peppers (optional, for heat)

-3 shallots

-1 green bell pepper

-Zest and juice of 1 lime

-2 tablespoons of brown sugar

-1 tablespoon of apple cider vinegar

-2 cloves of garlic

-½ bunch of cilantro or culantro

-½ tablespoon of black pepper

-Olive oil and salt to taste

Yields: 6 cups

Use for:

-Sauces

-Marinating and basting pork chops

-Fish and shrimp

Sofrito de Chipotle y Mora

While any species of blackberry can be used in this recipe, or even raspberries in a pinch, the intended fruit for this sofrito is the mora de Castilla, also known as the frambuesa Andina. It is a type of blackberry found throughout the South American Andes with a distinctly sweet and fruity flavor and aroma. Frozen Andean blackberry, or its pulp, can be found in many Latin markets in the U.S.

-2 cups of mora de Castilla or another type of blackberry or raspberry, or 12 oz of mora pulp.

-8 chipotle peppers or 1 small can of chipotles in adobo

-2 white onions

-8 cloves of garlic

-1 yellow or orange bell pepper

-1 tablespoon of naranja agria or zest of ½ an orange

-3-4 tablespoons of tamarind paste (optional)

-Olive oil and salt to taste

Yields: 6 cups

Use for:

-Marinating and basting pork chops

-Sauces

-Baked, grilled, or roasted chicken

Sofrito con Cerveza

Cook the alcohol out of a nice, dark beer to develop a complex flavor in this sofrito.

-1 yellow onion

-1 shallot

-1 red or green bell pepper

-1 bunch of cilantro

-1 bunch of green onions

-2 poblano peppers

-3 cloves of garlic

-Juice and zest of 1 lime

-1 tablespoon of soy sauce

-1 teaspoon of parsley

-1 ½ cups of dark beer

-Olive oil and salt to taste

Yields: 6-7 cups

Use for:

-Sauces

-Marinating and basting poultry

-Braised meat dishes

Super Hot Sofrito

This sofrito is not for the faint of heart. It adds a spicy punch to any dish.

-2 red onions

-8 cloves of garlic

-1 bunch of cilantro

-12 habanero peppers

-8 chipotle peppers or 1 small can of chipotles in adobo

-3 poblano peppers

-6 serrano peppers

-3 tablespoons of naranja agria

-1 teaspoon of apple cider vinegar

-1 8-oz jar of alcaparrado (or 1/3 cup olives, 1/3 cup capers, ¼ cup pimientos)

-Olive oil or lard and salt to taste

Yields: 6-7 cups

Use for:

-Sautéed vegetables

-Stewed meats

-Rice or beans

.

Roasted Red Pepper and Eggplant Sofrito

Roasted or grilled red peppers and eggplant lend a tasty umami flavor to this sofrito, which balances with the richness of butter or lard. Bacon can be added to this sofrito if desired.

-1 yellow onion

-3 red bell peppers, roasted

-2 eggplants

-10 cloves of garlic

-1 bunch of cilantro

-5 ají dulce peppers

-2 cubanelle peppers

-Juice of 1 lemon

-2 tablespoons of smoked paprika

-1 tablespoon of black pepper

-Butter or lard and salt to taste

Yields: 7-8 cups

Use for:

-Dips

-Soups and stews

-Sautéed vegetables

Carrot and Ginger Sofrito

This sofrito is a bit sweet and spicy, lending an exciting flavor to rice and pairing well with seafood.

- 1 red onion

- 1 shallot

- 1 ½ bunches of cilantro

- ½ of a red or yellow bell pepper

- 1 bunch of green onions

- 3 medium or 1-2 large carrots

- 3-4 tablespoons of minced or grated ginger

- 1 poblano pepper

- 3-4 jalapeño peppers (or serranos if more heat is preferred)

- 1.5 tablespoons of sugar

- 1 teaspoon of oregano

- Olive oil and salt to taste

Yields: 5 cups

Use for:

- Rice dishes

- Spoon over fish

- Sautéed shrimp

Green Tomato Sofrito

This sofrito is a great way to use green or unripe tomatoes, and its flavor is particularly versatile.

- 8 medium green tomatoes (or 4 very large ones)

- 1 bunch of cilantro or culantro

- 1 bunch of parsley

- 1 ½ green bell peppers

- ½ of a white or yellow onion

- 8 cloves of garlic

- 6 jalapeño peppers

- 1 tablespoon of honey

- 1 teaspoon of black pepper

- 1 teaspoon of smoked paprika

- 1 8-oz jar of alcaparrado (or 1/3 cup olives, 1/3 cup capers, ¼ cup pimientos) (optional)

- Olive oil and salt to taste

Yields: 7-8 cups

Use for:

- Soups and stews

- Rice and grains

- Beans and lentils

Citrusy Sofrito

This bright and citrus-forward sofrito is sure to be one of your favorites. Feel free to modify the recipe and use whatever citrus is in season or that you have access to- the fresher, the better.

-2 yellow onions

-1 bunch of cilantro or culantro

-1 bunch of parsley

-2 poblano peppers

-2 cubanelle peppers

-1 banana pepper

-1 red jalapeño or fresno chili

-Juice and zest of 2 oranges

-Juice and zest of 2 limes or lemons

-2 tablespoons of naranja agria

-2 tablespoons of ají amarillo paste (optional)

-1 tablespoon of mint (optional)

-1 teaspoon of minced or grated ginger (optional)

-1 tablespoon of honey

-Olive oil and salt to taste

Yields: 5-6 cups

Use for:

-Pan-fried seafood

-Marinating and basting poultry

-Rice dishes

Sofripesto

Pesto lovers will appreciate this basil-based sofrito with a Latin flair. Cashews are used in place of pine nuts due to their widespread use in Latin America and the Caribbean, and the way they pair beautifully with the other elements of this recipe. For a version containing meat, see page 61.

-2 cups of loose basil leaves, stems removed

-½ a bunch of cilantro

-2 shallots

-1.5 tablespoons of fresh oregano leaves (may substitute with 1 tablespoon of dried)

-5 cloves of garlic

-2 tablespoons of cashews

-½ of a green bell pepper

-Juice of ½ a lemon

-1 poblano pepper

-2 teaspoons of ají amarillo paste (optional)

-1 teaspoon of huacatay paste (optional)

-Olive oil and salt to taste

Yields: 2 cups

Use for:

-Poultry

-Sautéed shrimp

-Topping or garnishing dishes

Saffron and Mushroom Sofrito

A sofrito with delectable umami notes to build the most incredible savory dishes.

-4 shallots

-6 cloves of garlic

-1 ½ cups of mushrooms

-Juice of ½ a lemon

-1 red bell pepper

-1 carrot

-1 8-oz jar of alcaparrado (or 1/3 cup olives, 1/3 cup capers, ¼ cup pimientos)

-½ a bunch of culantro

-½ a bunch of parsley

-Juice of half a lemon

-6-8 saffron threads

-2 teaspoons of oregano

-1 teaspoon of black pepper

-Olive oil and salt to taste

Yields: 6-7 cups

Use for:

-Rice

-Stewed meats

-Stuffing pork or chicken

Pomegranate, Jalapeño, and Mint Sofrito

Refreshing mint and tangy pomegranate pair with jalapeños for a flavorful kick.

- 2 red onions

- 5 cloves of garlic

- ½ a green bell pepper

- ½ cup of pomegranate arils

- 1 bunch of cilantro or culantro

- Juice and zest of ½ a grapefruit or 1 small orange

- 2 teaspoons of fresh oregano (can substitute dried)

- ½ cup of fresh mint leaves

- 1 tablespoon of huacatay paste

- 8 jalapeños (may remove seeds if less spice is preferred)

- Olive oil and salt to taste

Yields: 5-6 cups

Use for:

- Sauces

- Quick sautéed meats

- Vegetables

Pineapple Sofrito

The sweet and sour flavor of pineapple gives this sofrito a tropical flair. Chop it very finely and cook it down well for best results.

-1 red onion

-6 cloves of garlic

-1 bunch of cilantro or culantro

-2/3 cup of pineapple

-1 green bell pepper

-4 jalapeño, serrano, or habanero peppers, depending on spice preference

-1 tablespoon of lime juice

-Olive oil and salt to taste

Yields: 4 cups

Use for:

-Rice

-Chicken

-Seafood

Sundried Tomato Sofrito

The practice of drying tomatoes in the sun is thought to have begun in Italy, but it is now used around the world and adds an interesting new flavor to traditional sofrito.

-1 cup of sundried tomatoes

-1 yellow onion

-2 tablespoons of tomato paste (use sundried tomato paste if available)

-1 bunch of cilantro

-1 bunch of parsley

-½ cup of fresh basil, stems removed

-10 cloves of garlic

-Leaves of 2 sprigs of thyme

-2 tablespoons of oregano, fresh or dried

-1 red or green bell pepper

- 1 8-oz jar of alcaparrado (or 1/3 cup olives, 1/3 cup capers, ¼ cup pimientos)

-¼ cup of white wine

-Olive oil and salt to taste

Yields: 6.5 cups

Use for:

-Stews

-Sauces

-Chicken

Caramelized Onion Sofrito

Caramelize the onions beforehand in butter for at least 8 hours, then add them to this delicious sofrito that is well worth the time.

-½ cup of caramelized onions (about a pound of onions when raw)

-½ bunch of cilantro

-5 ají dulce peppers or 2 cubanelle peppers

-5 cloves of garlic

-1 habanero pepper (optional)

-1 teaspoon of tomato paste or 1 tomato bouillon cube

-1 tablespoon of apple cider vinegar or sherry vinegar

-¼ cup of white wine or light beer (optional)

-Olive oil, butter, or lard and salt to taste

Yields: 2 cups

Use for:

-Potatoes

-Picadillo

-Topping, garnishing, or filling empanadas or quesadillas

Sofritos with Meat

In many regions, it's not uncommon for meat to be part of a sofrito, and in the vast majority of cases, it's pork. Some of the recipes from the previous section already offer lard as a delicious alternative to oil. These recipes take it a step further by incorporating cuts of meat to truly elevate the flavor. The sofrito can be stored using the same methods as before, and the meat is usually cut finely enough and in a small enough proportion that it can be blended in smoothly, though if the blending aspect poses a problem (perhaps due to a less powerful device), the pieces of meat can be added at the end to an already blended product, keeping them intact but making your sofrito less homogenous as a consequence.

Smoky Spanish Sofrito

Use smoked bacon in this sofrito to add more depth of flavor to the classic ingredients.

- 3 yellow onions

- 1 leek

- 1 red bell pepper

- 1 green bell pepper

- 8 cloves of garlic

- 4 medium fresh tomatoes or 2 cans

- 10 strips of smoked bacon, diced

- 1 cup of diced Spanish chorizo

- 3 tablespoons of tomato paste

- 2 tablespoons of oregano

- 1 tablespoon of parsley

- 2 tablespoons of lemon juice

- 4 tablespoons of smoked Spanish paprika

- 6 saffron threads (optional)

- 2 tablespoons of sherry vinegar

- 1 bay leaf, finely ground

- ¼ cup of vegetable stock or pork stock

- Leaves of 3 sprigs of thyme (or ½ tablespoon of dried thyme)

- Leaves of 3 sprigs of rosemary (or 1 tablespoon of dried rosemary)

- Celery salt, smoked salt, or sea salt to taste

Smoky Spanish Sofrito (cont.)

Yields: 10 cups

Use for:

-Stewed meats

-Paella

-Legumes

Sofrito for Beans

This Cuban-inspired sofrito is especially heavy in pork and makes a delicious addition to beans. The meat can be diced and added after the rest of the ingredients are blended.

-½ cup of diced ham

-1 cup of chorizo

-4 strips of smoked bacon

-3 medium tomatoes

-1 green bell pepper

-1 poblano pepper

-3 jalapeño or 1 serrano pepper

-2 tablespoons of tomato paste

-2 yellow onions

-10 cloves of garlic

-1 tablespoon of oregano

-1 teaspoon of smoked paprika

-2 bay leaves, finely ground

-Lard or olive oil and salt to taste

Yields: 8-9 cups

Use for:

-Beans

-Stews

-Add to scrambled eggs

Recaíto Especial

This is perhaps one of the best versions of recaíto, sure to pack lots of flavor into any dish.

- 3 yellow onions

- 1 bunch of cilantro

- 1 bunch of culantro

- 15 ají dulce peppers

- 1 green bell pepper

- 1 red bell pepper

- 1 whole head of garlic

- 6 strips of smoked bacon

- 1 cup of diced ham

- 1 tablespoon of achiote

- 1 8-oz jar of alcaparrado (or 1/3 cup olives, 1/3 cup capers, ¼ cup pimientos)

- 6 tablespoons of tomato paste

- 2 bay leaves, finely ground

- Lard or olive oil and salt to taste

Yields: 9 cups

Use for:

- Braised or stewed meats

- Picadillo

- Beans

Sofrito con Jamón y Achiote

This is yet another sofrito that pairs very well with beans, as well as any sort of stew. It is ideal to use lard for this recipe.

-1 yellow onion

-1 red bell pepper

-1 poblano pepper

-8 cloves of garlic

-½ bunch of cilantro

-2 tablespoons of oregano

-1 cup of diced ham

-2 tablespoons of achiote

-Lard or olive oil and salt to taste

Yields: 6 cups

Use for:

-Beans

-Stews

-Sauces

Smoky Aderezo

A variety of aderezo containing savory bacon pared with sweet and smoky chilies.

-1 red onion

-1 shallot

-4 cloves of garlic

-6 ají panca peppers or 2-3 tablespoons of ají panca paste

-10 ají chaparita peppers or 3 tablespoons of ají chaparita paste

-4 strips of smoked bacon

-1 teaspoon of coriander

-1 tablespoon of black mint paste (huacatay)

-Lard and salt to taste

Yields: 3 cups

Use for:

-White beans

-Rice dishes

-Marinades

Pumpkin and Ham Sofrito

Perfect for the fall, this sofrito makes for a deliciously hearty base to rice dishes like arroz con pollo, or for flavoring plain rice as a side.

- 1 small pumpkin (about 1-2 lbs) or 1 can of puree

- 2 yellow onions

- 1 ½ cups of diced smoked ham

- 6 cloves of garlic

- 1 bunch of cilantro

- 1 red or yellow bell pepper

- 2 ají amarillo peppers or 1 ½ tablespoons of paste

- 2 guajillo chilies

- Olive oil and salt to taste

Yields: 6.5 cups

Use for:

- Rice dishes

- Grains like quinoa

- Sautéed vegetables like corn

Sofrito with Espresso

One of the more complex flavor bases found in this book, this sofrito pairs pork and dried chilies with a touch of espresso and cocoa.

-1 yellow onion

-6 cloves of garlic

-1 red bell pepper

-Leaves of 4 sprigs of thyme

-3 strips of smoked bacon

-½ cup of diced ham

-3 guajillo chilies

-3 ancho chilies

-1 teaspoon of soy sauce

-1 tablespoon of smoked paprika

-1 teaspoon of oregano

-½ teaspoon of cinnamon

-½ teaspoon of cumin

-1 tablespoon of espresso

-1 teaspoon of dark unsweetened cocoa powder

-Butter or lard and salt to taste

Sofrito with Espresso (cont.)

Yields: 4 cups

Use for:

-Black or red beans

-Basting grilled meats

-Sauces

Spicy Sofripesto with Bacon

There may be no better way to improve the delicious sofripesto than with rich, smoky bacon. Serrano peppers add spice to this sofripesto to balance out the fats.

-1 yellow onion

-2 shallots

-3 poblano peppers

-8 serrano peppers

-3 cups of loose basil leaves, stems removed

-3 tablespoons of cashews

-1 bunch of cilantro

-6 strips of smoked bacon

-1 teaspoon of huacatay paste (optional)

-1 teaspoon of apple cider vinegar

-1 teaspoon of black pepper

-1 teaspoon of oregano

-Olive oil and salt to taste

Yields: 6 cups

Use for:

-Pasta

-Rub for grilled meats and poultry

-Sautéed vegetables

Grilled Corn and Epazote Sofrito

Epazote is an herb common in Mexican cooking that pairs well with the elements of this recipe. Grill or char the corn, red peppers, and jalapeños in this recipe to add a greater depth of flavor.

- Kernels from 4 ears of corn, grilled

- 2 red bell peppers, grilled

- 1 bunch of cilantro

- 2 red onions

- 1 cup of fresh epazote

- 4 strips of smoked bacon

- ¼ cup of smoked ham

- 5 jalapeños, grilled

- 2 teaspoons of achiote

- 1 teaspoon of oregano

- 1 teaspoon of lime juice

- Olive oil and salt to taste

Yields: 8 cups

Use for:

- Braised chicken

- Rice

- Beef Stew

Sofrito con Chorizo Mexicano

This sofrito incorporates savory Mexican chorizo for a fantastic flavor base. The fat in the chorizo eliminates the need for additional oil.

-1 pound of Mexican chorizo (pork or beef)

-12 cloves of garlic

-2 white or yellow onions

-4 medium tomatoes or equivalent in canned tomatoes or paste

-1 bunch of cilantro

-1 red bell pepper

-3 dried ancho chilies

-3 dried guajillo chilies

-1 tablespoon of apple cider vinegar

-Leaves of 3 sprigs of thyme

-1 teaspoon of cumin

-1 tablespoon of smoked paprika

-2 teaspoons of oregano

-1 teaspoon of black pepper

-1 tablespoon of achiote

-Salt to taste

Yields: 8 cups

Use for:

-Stuffing pork or chicken

-Beans

-Potatoes

Around the World

This section contains recipes for flavor bases closely related to sofrito. They are included in this book because of the way they have influenced or evolved alongside Spanish and Latin sofritos and can expand the way we combine flavors.

Green Seasoning

A staple in many parts of the Caribbean, green seasoning is a cousin of sofrito enjoyed in Jamaica, Trinidad, and other islands. It is spicy, flavorful, and great as a marinade for chicken or seafood.

- 1 white onion

- 1 bunch of green onions

- 1 bunch of cilantro

- ½ bunch of culantro

- 1 tablespoon of grated fresh ginger

- 1-2 scotch bonnets (can substitute habaneros or a handful of cubanelles); quantity can depend on spice preference, leave seeds in if a hotter product is desired.

- 1 stalk of celery, leaves and all

- 1 green bell pepper

- 1 bunch of parsley

- Leaves from 8 sprigs of thyme

- 2 tablespoons of basil

- 2 tablespoons of rosemary

- 1 tablespoon of oregano

- juice of 2 small limes (or 1 large)

- 1 whole head of garlic

- 1 bouillon cube (chicken or vegetable) or equivalent

- Salt and white vinegar to taste

Green Seasoning (cont.)

Yields: 8-10 cups

Use for:

-Marinating meats and seafood

-Basting grilled meats

-White rice

Ginisá

Ginisá is fundamental to Filipino cuisine and is closely related to Spanish sofrito.

-1 yellow or red onion

-8 cloves of garlic

-2 medium tomatoes

-Olive oil and salt to taste

Yields: 3 cups

Use for:

-Rice dishes

-Sauces

-Soups and stews

Italian Soffritto

A soffritto in traditional Italian cuisine consists of onions, celery and carrots.

-1 white onion

-3 medium carrots

-3 stalks of celery

-Olive oil or butter and salt to taste

Yields: 3 cups

Use for:

-Soups

-Sauces

-Braised meats

Basic Sofregit

Much like refogado, sofregit is cooked down to a thick and
flavorful paste. It is widely used in Catalonian cooking.
Additional tomato sauce can replace fresh tomatoes or vice versa.
Tomato paste can also be used.

-2 yellow onions

-5 tomatoes

-1 cup of tomato sauce

-Olive oil and salt to taste

Yields: 4 cups

Use for:

-Rice dishes

-Seafood dishes

-Fideuá

Sofregit Especial

This sofregit features a few extra ingredients that hit all the right taste buds.

- 1 yellow onion

- 1 shallot

- 1 leek

- 4 cloves of garlic

- 3 tomatoes

- 1 cup of tomato sauce

- 1 red bell pepper

- 1 cup of wax cap, milk cap, or chanterelle mushrooms, finely chopped

- Olive oil and salt to taste

Yields: 5-6 cups

Use for:

- Rice dishes

- Braised meats

- Seafood dishes

Mirepoix

One of the most recognizable flavor trios in the culinary world, mirepoix forms the foundation of countless French dishes. Like any good sofrito, it should be cooked down low and slow. Different cuts of pork can be added for a meaty version.

-1 yellow onion

-1 large carrot

-2 stalks of celery

-Butter or lard and salt to taste

Yields: 3 cups

Use for:

-Braised meats

-Sauces

-Soups and stocks

Pinçage

A special breed of Mirepoix in which tomato paste is added to deepen the flavor.

-1 yellow onion

-1 large carrot

-2 stalks of celery

-3 tablespoons of tomato paste

-Butter or lard and salt to taste

Yields: 3 cups

Use for:

-Sauces

-Braised meats

-Casseroles

Włoszczyzna

Włoszczyzna is a Polish flavor base inspired by Italian soffritto. It is particularly delicious in soups. These vegetables can be cooked down in an oil like most sofritos, but it is actually quite common to just boil in water them for a long time, like a vegetable stock.

-2 leeks

-1 celery root

-2 parsley roots

-1 bunch of parsley, including stems and leaves

-4 carrots

-2 bay leaves, finely ground

-2 cups of white cabbage leaves

-Celery salt to taste (or salt and a handful of celery leaves)

-1 tablespoon of whole allspice

Yields: 10 cups

Use for:

-Soups and stocks

-Sauces

-Braised meats

Suppengrün

This German flavor base, like Włoszczyzna, is ideal for making soups and broths. Celery stalks and leaves can be substituted for celery root in a pinch. After cooking, the vegetables can be left as a dice or can be puréed.

-1 celery root

-3 carrots

-2 leeks

-1 bunch of parsley, including leaves and stems

-Butter or olive oil and salt to taste

Yields: 4 cups

Use for:

-Soups and stocks

-Sauces

-Marinades

Cajun Trinity

There might be no culinary base more recognizable in the U.S. South than the Cajun trinity. It is versatile and delicious in a wide range of applications.

-1 small or medium yellow onion (if very large, use about half)

-1 green bell pepper

-2-3 stalks of celery

-Butter or lard and salt to taste

Yields: 3 cups

Use for:

-Gumbo

-Jambalaya

-Red beans and rice

Smazhennya/Zazharka

Used in traditional borsch, and featured prominently in Ukrainian and Russian cuisine.

- 2 yellow onions

- 3 carrots

- 1 red bell pepper

- 2 tablespoons of tomato paste

- 1 cup of beetroot

- 1 bay leaf, finely ground

- Butter or lard and salt/pepper to taste

Yields: 5-6 cups

Use for:

- Borsch

- Sauces

- Vinaigrettes and dressings

Duxelles

Mushrooms, herbs and shallots cooked down to a paste, French duxelles is included in this book because of its preparation and usage similar to a sofrito. Just like Latin sofritos, it can be frozen into cubes for later use.

-4 cups of mushrooms (any varieties, though a mixture of different kinds yields a more complex flavor, and wild mushrooms are preferred)

-Leaves of 6 sprigs of thyme

-1 tablespoon of parsley

-4 shallots, 2 onions, or a combination

-1 tablespoon of sherry

-Butter, salt and pepper to taste

Yields: 5 cups

Use for:

-Stuffing pastries or wellingtons

-Garnishing chicken or pork chops

-Sauces

Thai Red Curry Paste

It may come from the other side of the globe, but if you think about it, Thai curry pastes are not so different from sofritos in terms of application. At the very least, they deserve an honorable mention in this book. Add a couple tablespoons of turmeric to make a yellow curry paste.

-2 tablespoons of fermented shrimp paste

-10-20 red Thai chilies, depending on spice preference

-1 stalk of lemongrass

-½ cup of cilantro root or stems

-2 tablespoons of galangal or ginger

-1 shallot

-6 cloves of garlic

-Zest of one lime (ideally Makrut lime)

-1 teaspoon of cumin

-1 tablespoon of white peppercorns

-Salt and neutral oil to taste

Yields: 1 cup

Use for:

-Thai red curry

-Rub for pork, beef or chicken

-Soups

Thai Green Curry Paste

Thai green curry tends to be more spicy than red because of the natural heat of the green chilies. Of course, you can adjust the spice level according to your tastes.

-3 tablespoons of fermented shrimp paste

-10-20 Thai green chilies, depending on spice preference

-8 cloves of garlic

-2 shallots

-2 stalks of lemongrass

-1 cup of cilantro root or stems

-4 tablespoons of galangal or ginger

-Zest of one lime (ideally Makrut lime)

-½ cup of Thai basil leaves

-1 tablespoon of sugar

-1 teaspoon of cumin

-1 teaspoon of coriander

-1 tablespoon of white peppercorns

-Salt and neutral oil to taste

Yields: 2 cups

Use for:

-Thai green curry

-Marinating and cooking chicken

-Stir fries

Afterword

I hope that the sofritos in this book have served to broaden your horizons and introduce you to a world of Latin and Caribbean cooking. The flavors you have now created provide the foundation to a vast world of culinary delights, spanning dozens of countries and countless cultures. It is my desire that you have begun to explore new dishes and fun ways to use sofrito. Maybe you'll even develop your own special recipe. If you do, make sure to pass it on and share it with family- that's how beautiful traditions begin.